Donald Trump's Accomplishments...

Donald Trump's Accomplishments...

Donald Trump's Accomplishments...

Donald Trump's Accomplishments...

Donald Trump's Accomplishments...

Donald Trump's Accomplishments...

Donald Trump's Accomplishments...

Donald Trump's Accomplishments...

Donald Trump's Accomplishments...

Donald Trump's Accomplishments...

Donald Trump's Accomplishments...

Donald Trump's Accomplishments...

Donald Trump's Accomplishments...

Donald Trump's Accomplishments...

Donald Trump's Accomplishments...

Donald Trump's Accomplishments...

Donald Trump's Accomplishments...

Donald Trump's Accomplishments...

Donald Trump's Accomplishments...

Donald Trump's Accomplishments...

Donald Trump's Accomplishments...

Donald Trump's Accomplishments...

Donald Trump's Accomplishments...

Donald Trump's Accomplishments...

Donald Trump's Accomplishments...

Donald Trump's Accomplishments...

Donald Trump's Accomplishments...

Donald Trump's Accomplishments...

Donald Trump's Accomplishments...

Donald Trump's Accomplishments...

Donald Trump's Accomplishments...

Donald Trump's Accomplishments...

Donald Trump's Accomplishments...

Donald Trump's Accomplishments...

Donald Trump's Accomplishments...

Donald Trump's Accomplishments...

Donald Trump's Accomplishments...

Donald Trump's Accomplishments...

Donald Trump's Accomplishments...

Donald Trump's Accomplishments...

Donald Trump's Accomplishments...

Donald Trump's Accomplishments...

Donald Trump's Accomplishments...

Donald Trump's Accomplishments...

Donald Trump's Accomplishments...

Donald Trump's Accomplishments...

Donald Trump's Accomplishments...

Donald Trump's Accomplishments...

Donald Trump's Accomplishments...

Donald Trump's Accomplishments...

Donald Trump's Accomplishments...

Donald Trump's Accomplishments...

Donald Trump's Accomplishments...

Donald Trump's Accomplishments...

Donald Trump's Accomplishments...

Donald Trump's Accomplishments...

Donald Trump's Accomplishments...

Donald Trump's Accomplishments...

Donald Trump's Accomplishments...

Donald Trump's Accomplishments...

Donald Trump's Accomplishments...

Donald Trump's Accomplishments...

Donald Trump's Accomplishments...

Donald Trump's Accomplishments...

Donald Trump's Accomplishments...

Donald Trump's Accomplishments...

Donald Trump's Accomplishments...

Donald Trump's Accomplishments...

Donald Trump's Accomplishments...

Donald Trump's Accomplishments...

Donald Trump's Accomplishments...

Donald Trump's Accomplishments...

Donald Trump's Accomplishments...

Donald Trump's Accomplishments...

Donald Trump's Accomplishments...

Donald Trump's Accomplishments...

Donald Trump's Accomplishments...

Donald Trump's Accomplishments...

Donald Trump's Accomplishments...

Donald Trump's Accomplishments...

Donald Trump's Accomplishments...

Donald Trump's Accomplishments...

Donald Trump's Accomplishments...

Donald Trump's Accomplishments...

Donald Trump's Accomplishments...

Donald Trump's Accomplishments...

Donald Trump's Accomplishments...

Donald Trump's Accomplishments...

Donald Trump's Accomplishments...

Donald Trump's Accomplishments...

Donald Trump's Accomplishments...

Donald Trump's Accomplishments...

Donald Trump's Accomplishments...

Donald Trump's Accomplishments...

Donald Trump's Accomplishments...

Donald Trump's Accomplishments...

Donald Trump's Accomplishments...

Donald Trump's Accomplishments...

Donald Trump's Accomplishments...

Donald Trump's Accomplishments...